HYENAS

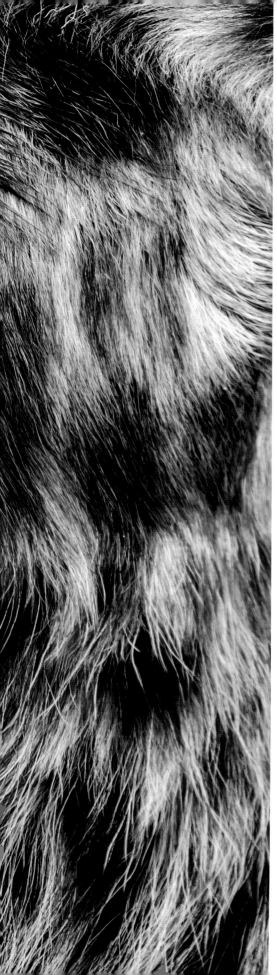

LIVING WILD

Published by Creative Education and Creative Paperbacks
P.O. Box 227, Mankato, Minnesota 56002
Creative Education and Creative Paperbacks are imprints of The Creative Company
www.thecreativecompany.us

Design and production by Mary Herrmann
Art direction by Rita Marshall
Printed in China

Photographs by Creative Commons Wikimedia (Bibliothèque nationale de France, Neil McIntosh/Flickr, Rigelus, Sémhur/Klaus D. Peter, South African Tourism/www.southafrica.net, Tiberio, US Army Africa/BDF Wildlife Training Area/Flickr), Dreamstime (Jeremy Brown), Getty Images (Barcroft Media, DEA/C. SAPPA/De Agostini), iStockphoto (cworthy, pjmalsbury, Richmatts), Shutterstock (Always take the shot, Bridgena BArnard, gualtiero boffi, Chad Wright Photography, e2dan, EcoPrint, Simon Eeman, Filipe.Lopes, GParker, Claude Huot, Petrovic Igor, Attila JANDI, Jarry, Vladislav T. Jirousek, Bill Livingstone, Lookingforcats, LouieLea, nattanan726, David Owen, Pearl Media, JT Platt, poylock19, Ondrej Prosicky, Rocket Photos, Maryna Shkvyria, Hannes Thirion, Evgenii Urlapov, Sergey Uryadnikov, Utopia_88, Cathy Withers-Clarke, John Wollwerth)

Photograph on p. 29 courtesy of Jean Clottes Photography.

Library of Congress Cataloging-in-Publication Data
Names: Gish, Melissa, author.
Title: Hyenas / Melissa Gish.
Series: Living wild.
Includes index.
Summary: A look at hyenas, including their habitats, physical characteristics such as their powerful jaws, behaviors, relationships with humans, and the declining populations of these often-misunderstood animals in the world today.
Identifiers: LCCN 2017035415 / ISBN 978-1-60818-958-8 (hardcover) / ISBN 978-1-62832-563-8 (pbk) / ISBN 978-1-64000-037-7 (eBook)

Subjects: LCSH: 1. Hyenas—Juvenile literature. 2. Hyenas—Behavior—Juvenile literature.
Classification: LCC QL737.C24 G57 2018 / DDC 599.74/3—dc23

CCSS: RI.5.1, 2, 3, 8; RST.6-8.1, 2, 5, 6, 8; RH.6-8.3, 4, 5, 6, 7, 8

First Edition HC 9 8 7 6 5 4 3 2 1
First Edition PBK 9 8 7 6 5 4 3 2 1

CREATIVE EDUCATION • CREATIVE PAPERBACKS

HYENAS

Melissa Gish

Nighttime darkness shrouds Kenya's Aberdare
National Park. A spotted hyena steps through

tall, dry grass, following the scent of blood.

Nighttime darkness shrouds Kenya's Aberdare National Park. A spotted hyena steps through tall, dry grass, following the scent of blood. The limp body of an antelope lies behind a fallen tree. Whooping, the hyena calls members of its clan to join in the feast. They whoop in response as they gather around the antelope, their powerful jaws prepared to rip flesh and crush bone. Suddenly, a lioness rushes in from the darkness. She roars and swipes a massive paw at the

nearest hyena. The hyenas' excited whooping turns into frantic yipping. They must work together. Several hyenas race around the lioness, distracting her from her kill. Two other hyenas grab the antelope and drag it into the grass. The lioness's paw catches one of the hyenas by the rump, but the agile hyena slips away. It follows its clan into the darkness, leaving the lioness searching for her meal. The hyenas will eat well tonight.

WHERE IN THE WORLD THEY LIVE

■ **Spotted Hyena**
sub-Saharan Africa

■ **Striped Hyena**
northern Africa
through the Middle
East to India

■ **Brown Hyena**
southern Africa

■ **Aardwolf**
southern and
eastern Africa

As they roam the savannas and arid regions of Africa and the Middle East, hyenas contribute to the health of their environments. Even with a global population of nearly 50,000, spotted hyenas may soon be in jeopardy, and all four hyena species' numbers are declining in the wild. This is spurring action among scientists to change people's misconceptions about these unique beasts. The colored squares represent regions where hyenas are still to be found in the wild today.

A MOTLEY MIX OF MAMMALS

The greatest number of brown hyenas can be found in the region of Africa's Kalahari Desert.

F our species of hyena make up the family Hyaenidae. Although hyenas are doglike in appearance, their ancestors were cats, and through the millennia, they have retained many catlike behaviors. The name "hyena" can be traced back to the ancient Greeks, who thought the hyena's mane of fur looked like the bristles on a wild pig's neck. They called the animal *hyaina*, from *hys*, meaning "pig," and *aina*, meaning "view." Each hyena species has earned various nicknames. The spotted hyena is called the laughing hyena because of its whooping call. It can be found throughout sub-Saharan Africa, with the exception of the Congo basin and southern South Africa. The striped hyena is nicknamed the Barbary hyena for its habitat along the Barbary Coast of Africa, from Morocco to Egypt. Striped hyenas can also be found across the Arabian Peninsula into the Middle East and as far east as central India. The brown hyena is known as the strand wolf in reference to its existence near the city of Strand in Western Cape, South Africa. Strand, the word for "beach" in the Afrikaans language, was established in 1714 and today is home to about 50,000 people. The brown hyena is also

Hyenas have acute hearing and can detect the sound of another animal killing or feeding on prey from up to six miles (9.7 km) away.

found throughout much of Namibia, Botswana, and South Africa. The fourth hyena species, the aardwolf, is named for the way it feeds. It licks up termites from mounds of earth. Its name means "earth wolf" in Afrikaans. Two populations of aardwolves exist. One ranges over most of South Africa into Angola, southern Zambia, and southwestern Mozambique. The other group extends from central Tanzania to northeastern Uganda and Somalia through Ethiopia and Sudan to southeastern Egypt.

Hyenas' rear legs are shorter than the front legs, so the rear end slopes downward. This prevents predators from getting a good grip on the hyena from behind. The four species have many more differences than similarities. Spotted hyenas are intelligent, powerful predators that hunt in packs to bring down large animals. Striped and brown hyenas are shy scavengers and hunters of small prey. And aardwolves survive by eating mostly insects. Each species is suited to its particular lifestyle.

The spotted hyena is the largest and most abundant hyena. It stands up to three feet (0.9 m) tall at the shoulder and measures about five feet (1.5 m) from muzzle to rump. Males can weigh up to 135 pounds (61.2 kg). Females

Northern and southern subspecies of aardwolf are classified by their geographical location on the African continent.

Two spotted hyenas working together to bring down prey are five times as successful as a hyena working alone.

typically weigh up to 190 pounds (86.2 kg). Spotted hyenas have short, rough, yellowish-brown fur with dark spots on the body. Dark brown fur covers the muzzle and the end of the bushy 12- to 14-inch (30.5–35.6 cm) tail. The legs can have spots, or they can be dark brown. The babies, called cubs, are born solid brown. When they are about three months old, cubs develop distinct spots. Spotted hyenas have short, bristly manes that run down the back of the neck. Their ears are rounded, and, like those of all hyena species, each paw has four clawed toes.

The spotted hyena's heart, which is twice as big as a lion's, makes up about 1 percent of its body weight. This gives spotted hyenas incredible stamina. They can run at a steady pace of about six miles (9.7 km) per hour for several hours, allowing them to exhaust prey to the point of collapse. They can also sprint at up to 35 miles (56.3 km) per hour, making their coordinated attacks highly successful. The spotted hyena's shoulders and neck are muscular and can withstand the twisting and pulling of prey trying to escape its bite. Powerful cheek and jaw muscles give spotted hyenas the strongest bite in relation to size of any animal on the planet. A 2,000-pound (907 kg) great white shark bites with

The spotted hyena's powerful upper body and jaws give it a distinct advantage over prey.

Mother spotted hyenas follow their young on their first hunts, teaching them strategies and making sure the prey does not escape.

Brown hyenas often eat a protein-rich fungus called the Kalahari truffle to supplement their diet.

690 pounds of pressure per square inch (48.5 kg/sq cm), or psi. Despite being 15 times smaller, a spotted hyena can bite with 700 psi (49.2 kg/sq cm).

The striped hyena varies greatly in size, depending on its geographic location. Those in the Middle East and Asia can weigh as much as 120 pounds (54.4 kg). Those in Africa typically weigh 60 to 80 pounds (27.2–36.3 kg). The ears are big and sharply pointed. The legs and body are gray with black stripes that are lighter in summer and darker in winter. The face and muzzle are dark, and a black patch covers the throat. A long mane running from the head to the rump stands up straight when the hyena is agitated. In winter, the mane can be nearly nine inches (22.9 cm) long. The brown hyena has a shaggy, dark brown coat and light brown legs with dark stripes. The neck is light brown, and the head and muzzle are dark. Like the striped hyena, it has a dark mane, bushy tail, and pointed ears. Brown hyenas average 90 pounds (40.8 kg), with females weighing slightly less than males.

Striped and brown hyenas are not as muscular as spotted hyenas, but their jaws are powerful enough to splinter bone. These species feed mostly on **carrion**,

Scavenging striped hyenas keep alert to sounds from other predators that may signal the presence of a kill.

Spotted hyena numbers are considered stable, with a population believed to exceed 47,000 individuals.

Spotted hyenas greet each other by lifting a hind leg and sniffing the other's underside to determine their rank in the clan.

supplementing their diet with vegetation, fruit, and small prey such as insects, rodents, and tortoises. The estimated population of striped hyenas is under 10,000. Fewer than 8,000 brown hyenas exist, making this species one of the rarest large carnivores in Africa. The International Union for Conservation of Nature (IUCN) lists both the striped and brown hyena as near threatened.

A more abundant hyena is the aardwolf. This animal looks like a miniature version of the striped hyena, though its face is more foxlike. Scientists once placed the aardwolf in its own family as a striped hyena **mimic**, but **genetic** evidence has shown that this animal is a true hyena. Like its striped cousin, the aardwolf has large, pointed ears and a long mane that extends from behind the head to the tip of its bushy tail. Unlike other hyenas, it weighs less than 30 pounds (13.6 kg) and feeds almost exclusively on insects and **larvae**. All four hyena species have long, sharp canine teeth, but the aardwolf lacks its cousins' sharp, scissor-like back teeth, called carnassials. Instead of tearing flesh and bone, aardwolves use their long, sticky tongues to lick up bugs that are mashed with their peg-like back teeth.

Aardwolves obtain moisture from the termites they consume, so they may go without drinking water for longer periods.

Once considered lazy scavengers, spotted hyenas are now known to be highly skilled and organized hunters.

SKILLED HUNTERS & SHY SCAVENGERS

The four hyena species differ greatly in their habits and behaviors. Spotted hyenas live in groups of up to 90 members. Called clans, these groups are organized into a **hierarchy** and led by a dominant female, called the alpha female. She organizes hunts and the defense of the clan's home range. Every hyena knows its place in the clan. The best food goes to higher-ranking members. Males rank lowest in a hyena clan and submit to the dominance of females. Even low-ranking females have power over males. None of the males in a clan is an offspring of any of the female clan members. Males leave their family when they are about two years old and arrive as strangers in other clans. This prevents **inbreeding**.

Spotted hyenas use a wide range of vocalizations. Their high-pitched whoops, grunts, yips, and whines each have precise meanings. The laughing sound expresses excitement or frustration, usually when hyenas call other clan members to a kill or await their turn to feed. Each spotted hyena has a unique voice. Other hyenas in the clan recognize the voice and know exactly which hyena is vocalizing, even as the animals' voices get more high-pitched with age.

Hyenas regularly watch the sky for descending vultures—a sure sign that a carcass is not far away.

Hyenas' sense of smell is so acute that they can detect the scent of carrion from up to 2.5 miles (4 km) away.

Contrary to popular belief, spotted hyenas scavenge or steal only about 5 percent of their food. These animals are indeed more successful hunters than lions. Often, lions are the ones stealing food from hyenas! One study conducted in Tanzania found that 80 percent of the animal **carcasses** eaten by lions were actually killed by spotted hyenas.

Brown hyenas also have a social hierarchy, but an alpha male and his mate control each clan. Four to six hyenas make up a clan. Brown hyenas are far less competitive than spotted hyenas. They defend their home range together and help each other raise cubs. Unlike spotted hyenas, which will hunt by day or night, brown hyenas are strictly nocturnal, or active at night. The clan gathers around a communal den site to rest during the day. At night, individuals forage alone for carrion from roadkill or leftovers from other predators. These hyenas are mostly silent. They communicate using scent markers. All four hyena species have anal pouches that can be turned outside their bodies to smear a paste-like substance on rocks and trees. Brown hyenas use this substance extensively to mark the boundaries of their home ranges as they patrol up to 30 miles (48.3 km) each night. They also chase intruders out of the area.

Hyenas must often contend with dangerously protective parents when trying to bring down young prey animals.

Striped hyenas are similarly silent and nocturnal. But these hyenas do not live in clans. While they tend to feed within a selected home range, they do not fight to defend it. Instead, striped hyenas roam alone or with a mate and simply avoid each other by scent marks. If they meet other hyenas in passing, they usually just keep moving. They may discourage other hyenas from touching a carcass by rubbing their face against the smelly flesh. They wear the scent like a sign that says, "That's mine."

Helpless aardwolf cubs spend their first six to eight weeks in the family den, where both parents care for them.

Aardwolves do not live in clans, and they neither hunt nor scavenge. They eat insects and larvae. They prefer termites, which are the most protein-rich insects. Aardwolves typically visit up to 30 termite mounds a day, gobbling upwards of 300,000 insects. They never destroy a food source. Instead, they give each colony about a month to rebuild itself before returning to feed. Aardwolves have home ranges, but they typically share with other aardwolves, only chasing intruders away from their den sites. An aardwolf lives with its mate and young offspring. During the day, the family sleeps together in an underground burrow. At night, they forage alone. In the coldest part of winter, aardwolves forage in daylight and sleep at night to conserve energy.

All hyenas give birth inside dens, but they do not dig their own dens. They take over the dens of other animals or simply use rocky crevices. Hyenas' **gestation** period is three to four months. Other aspects of reproduction vary by species.

Scientists have determined that spotted hyenas have the most painful and difficult birth of any animal. Female spotted hyenas have unusual external reproductive organs that are long and narrow. The stretching that occurs during birth can result in cubs getting stuck and suffocating. The organ can also tear, causing the mother to bleed to death. About 25 percent of first-time mothers die, and 60 percent of firstborn cubs are stillborn. Females that successfully give birth have less difficulty with subsequent births. Usually one or two cubs are born. They weigh from 2 to 3.5 pounds (0.9–1.6 kg) at birth. Unlike other hyenas, which have enough nipples for all offspring, spotted hyenas have just two nipples. Born with their eyes open and their mouths

Prague Zoo in the Czech Republic has been breeding brown hyenas in captivity since 1967.

Hyenas can live well into their 20s in captivity, though their lives are rarely more than half this long in the wild.

The dominant female's juvenile offspring outrank the adults on lower levels of a clan's hierarchy.

Hyena cubs may nurse for two to three hours, filling up on milk so rich with fat and protein that they may go several days between feedings.

full of teeth, spotted hyena cubs immediately begin fighting for survival. Often, the stronger cub will either prevent the weaker cub from feeding or kill it outright. Within weeks of birth, a quarter of spotted hyena cubs that are born will perish. If food is in short supply, the alpha female may kill other females' cubs to ensure the survival of her own offspring. However, on rare occasions, hyena mothers will feed each other's cubs and may even adopt orphaned cubs. The cubs grow quickly, first chewing on sticks to strengthen their jaw muscles and then graduating to bones within a few months.

Brown hyenas give birth to up to five cubs in the fall. Usually only the alpha female breeds, but if a daughter has cubs, the females will share mothering duties. Striped hyenas produce one to four cubs either in spring or fall. Brown and striped hyena cubs are born blind and toothless, weighing about 1.5 pounds (0.7 kg). Aardwolves produce two to five cubs in November or December, when termites are most active. Born with their eyes open, these cubs weigh less than a can of soda.

Unlike those of spotted hyenas, cubs of the other three hyena species grow teeth when they are about two

weeks old. Spotted, striped, and brown hyena cubs begin to eat meat when they are about one month old. They may not be **weaned** until they are 12 to 18 months old. Aardwolf cubs grow faster than their larger cousins. They start eating insects and larvae at three months old and are weaned a month later. All male hyenas leave their parents around age two. Female spotted and brown hyenas may stay in their clan.

In spotted hyena society, dominant females raise their female pups to one day take over clan leadership.

About 4,300 years ago, images of hyenas were included in carvings on a tomb wall in the burial grounds of Saqqara, Egypt.

FIXING A FALSE REPUTATION

D epictions of hyenas go back more than 40,000 years to the earliest days of human **culture**, when people began painting and etching images on cave walls. Cave art appears around the world, but images of hyenas have been found only in France, where a subspecies of spotted hyena called the cave hyena was common. It weighed about 225 pounds (102 kg) and likely competed with prehistoric humans for food. Perhaps the most famous cave hyena image was found among hundreds of animals painted on the walls of Chauvet-Pont-d'Arc Cave in southeastern France. The hyena painting, stout and covered with spots, remained hidden for about 32,000 years before being discovered in 1994.

A cave hyena was also painted on a wall in the world-famous Lascaux caves. Though the neck is much longer than a real hyena's, the spots and stiff mane are unmistakably those of a hyena. Abri de la Madeleine, a deep crevice under a cliff in southwestern France, is another site that links humans and hyenas. Used as a shelter by prehistoric humans, the site was filled with artifacts when its discovery was recorded in 1875. One

The red-clay painting of a hyena in France's Chauvet Cave was made about 30,000 years ago.

In 1904, the emperor of Ethiopia sent a spotted hyena cub to president Theodore Roosevelt, who donated it to the National Zoo.

The carved spur along the bottom of the Creeping Hyena indicates its use as a spear-thrower, or atlatl.

artifact that is now housed in a French museum is part of an atlatl (*at-LAT-uhl*), a tool used to propel hunting darts faster and farther than by hand alone. The artifact, nicknamed the Creeping Hyena, was carved from a mammoth tusk between 17,000 and 12,000 years ago. It is about four inches (10.2 cm) long and highly detailed in the hyena's face. The Creeping Hyena is on display at the National Prehistoric Museum in Les Eyzies-de-Tayac-Sireuil, France. Hyenas are rare in prehistoric artwork, probably, as **anthropologists** suggest, because they were not liked or even respected by early humans.

In the days of the Egyptian rulers known as pharaohs, hyenas were definitely not a favored animal. Relics from ancient Egyptian cities and tombs show that hyenas were hunted for sport or food. From about 1550 to 1080 B.C., artists who worked for the pharaohs lived in Deir el-Medina. One of the relics found there was a piece of limestone featuring a striped hyena being hunted down by three dogs.

Over the centuries, hyenas have been misrepresented both in their physical features and their nature. Leo Africanus, who wrote a history and description of North Africa in 1550, said that hyenas had the body of a wolf

A hyena statue rests atop the Animal Wall at Cardiff Castle, which was added to the 11th-century castle in the late 1800s.

and the legs and feet of a human. Swiss naturalist Conrad Gesner, who wrote a five-volume illustrated history of animals, described hyenas as disgusting animals that dig bodies out of graves to devour them.

Between 1764 and 1767, the rural French town of Gévaudan was terrorized by an unidentified beast that roamed the countryside. It is reputed to have attacked, dismembered, and partially devoured more than 100 people. It was described as reddish in color with a thick, dark mane running the length of its back. No one knew exactly what kind of animal it was. King Louis XV offered a reward for the killing of the mysterious creature, dubbed *La bête du Gévaudan* (the Beast of Gévaudan). The

FROM THE HYENA

In the mysterious way that news travels in Africa, and which white men so seldom hear of, we learned that Senecoza and a minor chief had had a falling out of some kind. It was vague and seemed to have no especial basis of fact. But shortly afterward that chief was found half-devoured by hyenas. That, in itself, was not unusual, but the fright with which the natives heard the news was. The chief was nothing to them; in fact he was something of a villain, but his killing seemed to inspire them with a fright that was little short of homicidal....

Not long thereafter, ... I had ridden far out on the veldt, accompanied by my servant. As we paused to rest our horses close to a kopje, I saw, upon the top, a hyena eyeing us. Rather surprised, for the beasts are not in the habit of thus boldly approaching man in the daytime, I raised my rifle and was taking a steady aim, for I always hated the things, when my servant caught my arm.

"No shoot, *bwana*! No shoot!" he exclaimed hastily, jabbering a great deal in his own language, with which I was not familiar.

"What's up?" I asked impatiently.

He kept on jabbering and pulling my arm, until I gathered that the hyena was a fetish-beast of some kind.

"Oh, all right," I conceded, lowering my rifle just as the hyena turned and sauntered out of sight.

Something about the lank, repulsive beast and his shambling yet gracefully lithe walk struck my sense of humor with a ludicrous comparison.

Laughing, I pointed toward the beast and said, "That fellow looks like a hyena-imitation of Senecoza, the fetish-man." My simple statement seemed to throw the native into a more abject fear than ever.

by Robert E. Howard (1906–36)

An 18th-century engraving bears witness to how the Beast of Gévaudan was portrayed in contemporary accounts.

legend of the Beast has endured, and, recently, the hyena was pegged as a possible culprit. In 2009, a show on the History Channel suggested that the beast was a type of long-haired hyena. **Zoologists** disagree with this theory. It was more likely an entire pack of wolves, several of which were killed by a farmer named Jean Chastel, who is credited with ending the reign of the Beast. But the 2016 book *Beast: Werewolves, Serial Killers, and Man-Eaters: The Mystery of the Monsters of the Gévaudan*, by Gustavo Sánchez Romero and S. R. Schwalb, does not let the hyena off the hook entirely. The authors suggest that a hyena ran with the pack of wolves, inspiring them to be exceptionally bold and vicious. Though zoologists dismiss this theory as well, it seems hyenas now have a firm place in the **mythology** of the Beast of Gévaudan.

Not all reports of hyenas depict them as vicious killers. In fact, many descriptions of hyenas go too far in the opposite direction. Ernest P. Walker's 1964 three-volume *Mammals of the World* is still cited as an authoritative source, yet it describes the spotted hyena as cowardly and unwilling to defend itself. Until the late 1970s, even the *Encyclopaedia Britannica* labeled striped hyenas as cowards.

A Duke University study tested spotted hyena versus chimpanzee problem-solving with tasks requiring teamwork; the hyenas came out on top.

In truth, hyenas will fight fiercely to defend their offspring, clan, and food. Hyenas' intelligence has also been misrepresented. Disney's 1994 animated film *The Lion King* depicts three spotted hyena characters, Banzai, Ed, and Shenzi, as sneaky, rather stupid animals who align themselves with the evil lion Scar, who says of the hyenas, "I'm surrounded by idiots." Retellings of African folk tales, such as Mwenye Hadithi's book *Hungry Hyena* (1994), Judy Sierra's *The Mean Hyena* (1997), and Madafo Lloyd Wilson's *The Greedy Hyena* (2007), illustrate the ways people once believed hyenas behaved.

Recent television shows have helped to improve the hyena's reputation. Famous chimpanzee scientist Jane Goodall said that if she had the chance to spend another lifetime studying a different animal, it would be the hyena. She believes they are some of the most intelligent creatures on the planet. Wildlife biologist and conservationist Jeff Corwin agrees. He discussed spotted hyenas on an episode of the Animal Planet show *The Jeff Corwin Experience*. In "Kenya: Hyena, Queen of the Beasts" (2003), Corwin featured the work of Michigan State University's Mara Hyena Project. Kevin Richardson, who is known as "The

Lion Whisperer," is also a fan of hyenas. He is a South African animal behaviorist who has raised spotted hyenas from cubs and found them to be affectionate, social, and extremely smart. Richardson documented his experiences with spotted hyenas in "Growing Up Hyena," part of a 2005 Animal Planet series about the first year of an animal's life. Revealing the truth about hyenas will help people see them for what they really are: fascinating, intelligent animals with unique lives.

Kevin Richardson's wildlife sanctuary is home to spotted and striped hyenas, lions, and black leopards.

Researchers point to spotted hyenas as evidence that intelligence in mammals may have evolved in response to social behaviors.

UNCOVERING HYENA MYSTERIES

The giant short-faced hyena anatomically resembled modern hyenas but was a much larger carnivore.

A lower-ranking hyena will flatten its ears backward and bob its head to demonstrate submission to higher-ranking hyenas.

S cientists think all carnivores share a common ancestor, *Miacis cognitus*. This tree-dwelling, weaselly mammal existed about 60 million years ago. It eventually gave rise to two main groups of animals: Caniformia (ground-dwelling dogs and bears) and Feliformia (tree-dwelling cats and mongooses). Hyenas **evolved** as Feliforms, making them more closely related to cats than dogs. The first hyenas emerged about 15 million years ago. They looked nothing like modern hyenas. *Protictitherium gaillardi* was a ferret-sized, tree-dwelling creature with **retractable** claws. Gradually, hyenas grew bigger, came down from the trees, and lost their retractable claws.

By about 3 million years ago, hyenas had become enormous predators that shared the world with saber-toothed cats. *Pachycrocuta brevirostris*, also known as the giant short-faced hyena, dominated the **food chain**. The largest hyena ever known, it was twice as big as modern hyenas, standing up to 39 inches (99.1 cm) tall at the shoulder and weighing about 420 pounds (191 kg). It roamed in packs and scavenged the remains of saber-toothed cats' kills. Its

During winter in southern Africa, food shortages can cause aardwolves to lose up to 20 percent of their body weight.

jaws could crush elephant bones, and it devoured more than 50 pounds (22.7 kg) of meat every day.

Since the early 1990s, a team of researchers led by **paleontologist** Dr. Paul Palmqvist has been studying a collection of nearly 6,000 mammal fossils discovered in a cave near the Spanish village of Venta Micena. Palmqvist believes the cave served as a den for a clan of giant short-faced hyenas about 1.3 million ago. The fossil discovery may explain the relationship between hyenas and early humans. About 1.4 million years ago, a group of prehistoric humans called *Homo antecessor* became the first **hominids** to travel from Africa to southern Europe. But instead of continuing to spread across Europe, most traveled no farther than present-day Spain, likely because of the hyenas.

The work of Dr. Joan Madurell-Malapeira, from the Catalan Institute of Paleontology at the Autonomous University of Barcelona, supports this theory. Since *Homo antecessor* had not yet developed weapons for hunting, they had to compete for scavenged food with the giant short-faced hyena—and they usually lost. *Homo antecessor* died out about 800,000 years ago, but the giant short-faced hyena did not disappear until about 400,000 years later,

when **climate change**, the growing diversity of large predators, and possibly the introduction of another group of prehistoric humans, called Denisovans, altered their habitat. Smaller hyena species survived and moved south to Africa, where they evolved into modern hyenas.

Hyenas today respond differently to changes in their environment. Unlike many animals that are **displaced** or killed by habitat destruction, the burning of grassland and grazing of livestock that occurs in aardwolf habitats actually contributes to the *survival* of this species. Prescribed burns are set to encourage growth of stronger grass and plants. But until the new vegetation grows, harvester termites become more abundant on the barren

Controlled burning of savannas contributes to the healthy growth of new plants and grasses in aardwolf habitat.

Naturally cautious but also highly curious, hyenas tend to carefully inspect changes in their environment.

land. These insects provide aardwolves with a welcome food source. Spotted hyenas are **adaptable**, too, but they have not been able to avoid their greatest threat: humans. Spotted hyenas are considered abundant in Africa and not recognized as a threatened species. However, their population has been declining—even in some protected reserves—because they are routinely poisoned, trapped, and shot. They are frequently blamed for livestock losses, and in some places, they are killed for their body parts, which are used in folk medicines or even eaten.

Decades of research on spotted hyenas has continued

through the Holekamp Lab at Michigan State University in East Lansing. Teams of researchers working in Africa use a variety of methods to study the animals. They may tranquilize the hyenas to make them fall asleep. Then they can take blood samples to catalog the genetic makeup of clans. Sometimes collars holding **Global Positioning System** (GPS) tracking devices are placed around hyenas' necks. The GPS transmitters allow researchers to monitor the animals' movements. Stories, pictures, and videos about the researchers' work are shared regularly at msuhyenas .blogspot.com. The IUCN's Hyena Specialist Group recognizes that, while spotted hyenas number well above 10,000 individuals, keeping these animals inside protected national parks and reserves as well as continuing to gather information on hyena behavior and reproduction are vital to ensure their survival.

Unlike aardwolves and spotted hyenas, striped hyenas do not adapt well to changes in their habitats. Human actions that **encroach** on striped hyenas' home ranges lead to food shortages, declines in breeding, and increased conflicts with humans. Dr. Aaron P. Wagner of Michigan State University leads a team of researchers that have

Captive hyenas are given puzzles and other activities to encourage their inquisitive nature and help prevent boredom.

A hyena can consume up to a third of its own body weight in one feeding, absorbing every nutrient possible.

partnered with the Oregon Zoo, the Living Desert in California, and London's People's Trust for Endangered Species to study striped hyenas in Kenya. Striped hyena research is fairly new; Wagner suggests that the lack of knowledge about the striped hyena's behavior and reproduction explains why conservation plans are lacking for this species. Until researchers understand what striped hyenas need to survive in changing habitats, it is virtually impossible to do anything to help them. The first step, Wagner believes, is improving the way striped hyenas are viewed by the public. Scavenging hyenas are vital to their **ecosystems** because they help clean up dead and rotting animal carcasses. Until their unique value is recognized, people are unlikely to care enough about striped hyenas to consider conservation measures.

Brown hyenas suffer a similar problem. Their biggest threat comes from farmers and ranchers who blame them for livestock deaths. When ranchers come upon brown hyenas gnawing on dead sheep or calves, they assume the hyena did the killing. But brown hyenas rarely kill—they mostly scavenge. Educating local people about brown hyenas and gaining more knowledge about this rare

animal are goals for Dr. Ingrid Wiesel, the director of the Brown Hyena Research Project in Namibia. Wiesel also helped South Africa's Tswalu Kalahari Reserve start a brown hyena research program. Using motion-sensitive cameras that snap a picture when something moves in front of the lens, the program has captured images of brown hyenas' behavior in the wild. Understanding how all four hyena species use their habitats and interact with other wildlife will help scientists and conservationists develop plans to help hyenas thrive. Dispelling myths and educating people about hyenas are equally important if we hope to have hyenas around for generations to come.

Hyenas may try to catch vultures, flamingos, or other birds, if they need to find a quick meal.

ANIMAL TALE: HYENA, BRINGER OF DEATH

The hyena takes many forms in the folkore of various African cultures. Some stories portray the hyena as cowardly and deceitful, while others depict him as fierce and wise. In this tale from the Zulu, a people of South Africa, the hyena takes on the role of a god's messenger.

Unkulunkulu, the Great One, created all things, from the smallest grain of sand to the largest elephant. He made the first people, too, and set them upon the land to hunt animals and gather seeds and collect water from the river. Because the people used their resources wisely, Unkulunkulu decided to bestow upon them the gift of immortality. He called on Eagle to take the message to the people.

Eagle delivered the news, and even the oldest people did not die. Many generations of people lived on. As time passed, it became difficult to hunt enough animals, gather enough seeds, and collect enough water for all the people. Unkulunkulu became concerned. He called on Chameleon. "There are not enough resources for so many people," he said to Chameleon. "Go tell them that they can no longer live forever."

Chameleon set off across the land toward the place where the people lived. But soon he became thirsty, so he stopped at a pool to drink. Then he felt hungry, so he climbed a tree and hunted grasshoppers. Before long, he felt tired. *I will rest for a few minutes,* Chameleon thought, *and then I will deliver the news from Unkulunkulu.* But Chameleon fell asleep. By the time he awoke, he had forgotten all about Unkulunkulu's message for the people.

More time passed, and Unkulunkulu saw that all the people were still alive and struggling to feed themselves. He went to Chameleon. "Did you not deliver my message?" he asked. Chameleon confessed that he had not.

Unkulunkulu was angry. He told Chameleon to go into the forest and hide for the rest of his life. Then Unkulunkulu called on Hyena. "There are not enough resources for the people," he said to Hyena. "Go tell the people they can no longer live forever."

Hyena set off across the land toward the place where the people lived. Soon, he became thirsty, but he did not stop. Then he felt hungry, but again, he pushed the thought from his mind. He felt tired. *I cannot rest,* Hyena thought, *I must first tell the people the news from Unkulunkulu.* So Hyena kept traveling as the sun set.

Hyena arrived at the place where the people lived, just as the moon reached the center of the starlit sky. "I bring you news from Unkulunkulu," he called. "You will no longer be immortal." But the people were sleeping. Hyena called out again, this time a little louder: "Unkulunkulu has taken away your immortality." Still the village was quiet. Finally, Hyena barked and screamed to awaken the people. When they came out of their houses, the people saw the shadowy figure of Hyena in the moonlight. Thirsty, hungry, and exhausted, Hyena cried out, "You are all going to die!" And then he disappeared into the tall grass to find water and food and take a nap.

To this day, when people see Hyena, they are fearful of his power because they believe that he alone bestowed death upon all people.

GLOSSARY

adaptable – having the ability to change to improve one's chances of survival in an environment

anthropologists – scientists who study the history of humankind

carcasses – the dead bodies of animals

carrion – the rotting flesh of an animal

climate change – the gradual increase in Earth's temperature that causes changes in the planet's atmosphere, environments, and long-term weather conditions

culture – a particular group in a society that shares behaviors and characteristics that are accepted as normal by that group

displaced – forced to leave one's home due to destruction or disaster

ecosystems – communities of organisms that live together in environments

encroach – move into an area already occupied

evolved – gradually developed into a new form

food chain – a system in nature in which living things are dependent on each other for food

genetic – relating to genes, the basic physical units of heredity

gestation – the period of time it takes a baby to develop inside its mother's womb

Global Positioning System – a system of satellites, computers, and other electronic devices that work together to determine the location of objects or living things that carry a trackable device

hierarchy – a system in which people, animals, or things are ranked in importance one above another

hominids – a family of primates that walk on two feet, including humans and their extinct ancestors

inbreeding – the mating of individuals that are closely related; it can result in having offspring with health problems

larvae – the newly hatched, wingless, often wormlike form of many insects before they become adults

mimic – an organism that imitates the appearance of another organism

mythology – a collection of myths, or popular, traditional beliefs or stories that explain how something came to be or that are associated with a person or object

paleontologist – a scientist who studies fossils of animals, plants, and other organisms that existed long ago

retractable – able to be drawn in from an extended position

weaned – made the young of a mammal accept food other than nursing milk

zoologists – people who study animals and their lives

SELECTED BIBLIOGRAPHY

Baynes-Rock, Marcus. *Among the Bone Eaters: Encounters with Hyenas in Harar*. University Park: Pennsylvania State University, 2015.

Brottman, Mikita. *Hyena*. London: Reaktion Books, 2012.

Nicholls, Henry. "The Truth About Spotted Hyenas." BBC Earth. http://www.bbc.com/earth/story/20141028-the-truth -about-spotted-hyenas.

Schmidtke, Mike. "*Hyaena brunnea*." Animal Diversity Web. http://animaldiversity.org/accounts/Hyaena_brunnea/.

"Striped Hyena – *Hyaena hyaena*." San Diego Zoo Animals & Plants. http://animals.sandiegozoo.org/animals /striped-hyena.

Stump, Meghan. "*Proteles cristata* – Aardwolf." Animal Diversity Web. http://animaldiversity.org/accounts /Proteles_cristata/.

Note: Every effort has been made to ensure that any websites listed above were active at the time of publication. However, because of the nature of the Internet, it is impossible to guarantee that these sites will remain active indefinitely or that their contents will not be altered.

Spotted hyenas are strong swimmers and often take a dip to cool off and remove flies from their bodies.

INDEX